You are
good at

This Book
is
Written By
_____

I love
when you
cook

_____

_____

_____

_____

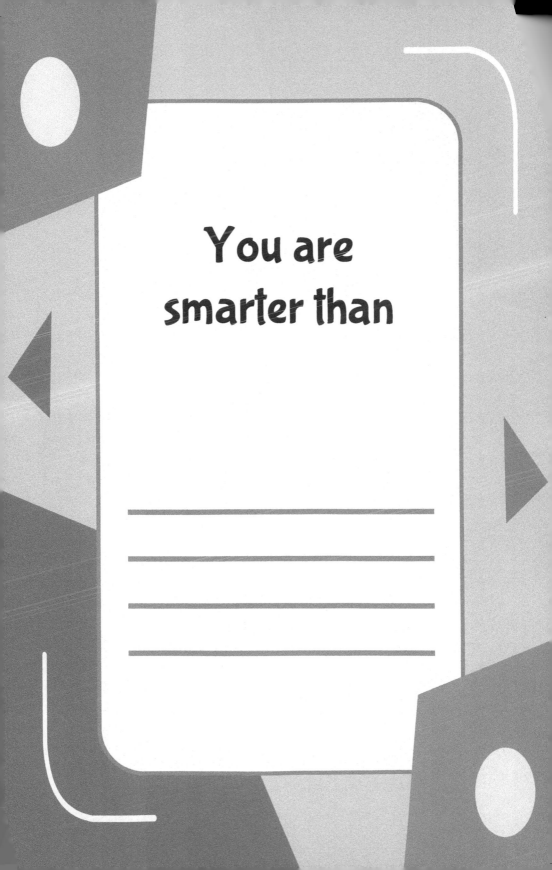

You are
smarter than

_____

_____

_____

_____

My favorite thing about you is

_____

_____

_____

_____

If I had million bucks I would buy you

_____

_____

_____

_____

Our favorite thing to do together is

_____

_____

_____

_____

You are the happiest when

_____

_____

_____

_____

Your favorite food is

_____

_____

_____

_____

Movie/TV show that we both love is

_____

_____

_____

_____

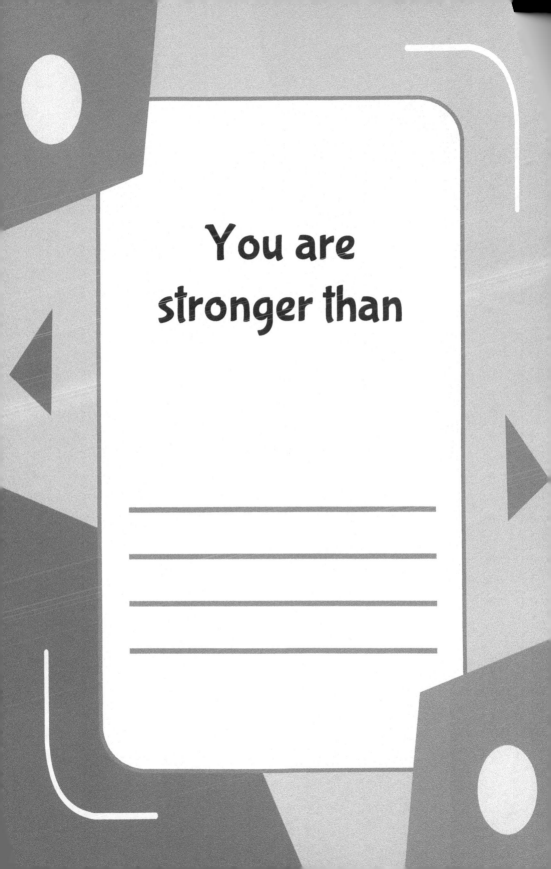

You are stronger than

_____

_____

_____

_____

You are special to me because

_____

_____

_____

_____

You make everyone

_____

_____

_____

_____

You
taught me
how to

_____

_____

_____

_____

I love
when you tell stories about

_____

_____

_____

_____

You
inspire me
to do

_____

_____

_____

_____

I enjoyed a lot when we went to

_____

_____

_____

_____

I love
when we prank

_____

_____

_____

_____

I love you a lot
because
you never

_____

_____

_____

_____

Funniest thing you do is

_____

_____

_____

_____

I
wish we have
more time to

_____

_____

_____

_____

I feel safe when you

_____

_____

_____

_____

You don't care about

I like when you make funny

_____

_____

_____

_____

I loved when you surprised me with

_____

_____

_____

_____

I love you more than

Game I like to play with you is

_____

_____

_____

_____

You are proud of me when I

_____

_____

_____

_____

I want you to know that I will

_____

_____

_____

_____